Best Of JOE SATRIANI

Photography by Neil Zlozower

CONTENTS

PERFORMANCE NOTES

ALWAYS WITH ME, ALWAYS WITH YOU

This lyrical ballad in 3/4 shows Joe as an evolved melodicist with sensitive phrasing abilities. Observe all the techniques Joe uses to bring out the melody, beginning at the melody's entrance: slides, vibratos, harmonics, bends and reverse bends. All of these he uses to coax the melody out of the guitar. During the relative-minor section (1:04) he plays a section of rapid rhythms connected by slurs. Like the slides in the first part, the slurs help effect a fluid sound from the lines; you never get the feeling that he's working very hard to achieve this texture. Even at the tapping section (1:52), where his virtuosity shines through, the notes don't sound forced. The bona fide guitar solo at 2:12 recalls another lyric virtuoso, Eric Johnson, with its soaring, major scale–based lines and even, effortless articulations.

BIG BAD MOON

After the ZZ Top–like groove, which provides the backdrop for the verses, Joe launches into two successive repeated-note motifs for the first guitar solo (0:58). Joe favors the top three strings for each phrase, descending to lower strings only at the tail ends of these phrases. This is a great way to build tension, and has been the favorite trick of such passionate players as Jimmy Page, Eddie Van Halen, and Stevie Ray Vaughan. The climax of this first solo occurs at 1:21, in the form of the minor-3rd trill. Joe's clear, brilliant tone and intelligibility are due in part to him using the pick edge to execute the trill.

At 2:31 we're treated to a Joe Satriani slide solo, where he emulates a harmonica by "dipping" sustained notes. To do this, he pulls the slide back on the fretboard and gradually comes back up to pitch. Rhythmic frenzy is what's in store for Guitar solo III, where Joe tears through a blistering pull-off and tapping cadenza for five bars, beginning at bar 10. It's a complete blur, rhythmically. Note the triplet brackets above the note groupings; these indicate that the three beats below each bracket must be played in the space of two beats.

CIRCLES

Joe starts off with some haunting sounds, but it is the ripping guitar solo that distinguishes this piece. At the double-time section at 2:31, Joe plays what might be the most "Van Halen–like" solo is his repertoire. Blues figures, wah machinations, irregular tuplet groupings and extended tapping passages are all invoked here. The rake picking at 2:51 offers the only respite in this otherwise blazing fusillade of notes.

THE CRUSH OF LOVE

Here's a terrific medium-tempo rocker in A minor, where Joe displays both his melodic and improvisational skills. The song is comprised of two basic melodic statements, one beginning on an A minor chord, the other on Fmaj7/A. He opens with the first statement, which he plays unadorned. The second statement begins with an ascending quarter-note triplet. Notice when this statement recurs its first note is always punctuated by a pronounced bar dip. This gives the opening note an expectorant, almost explosive quality. Between the melodic statements are burst of A minor glory, such as the descending figure at 1:56. Note that it's entirely A pentatonic minor (A C D E G), except for the choice placement of the blue $\flat5$ (E$\flat$) at the end of the second bar.

CRYIN'

Here Joe is melodic and expressive, so much so that you wonder if there aren't lyrics that accompany the instrumental version heard here. This is Joe's most restrained, least improvisatory song, and he allows only a hint of virtuosity to escape now and then. The first phrase shows just how many techniques Joe can bring to bear for a single melodic phrase: reverse bends, pull-offs, compound bends, vibratos, slides, and grace notes. He plays a fast, low-note flourish that he varies to great effect at 3:09. Never did an open low-E sound so satisfying as when it arrives precisely at the downbeat of the last measure of these busy figures.

FLYING IN A BLUE DREAM

Textural and atmospheric describe this song's opening, like the dream-like experience implied by the title. Joe introduces a hummable melody soon after the bass and drums kick in. That doesn't last for long, however, as soon we are thrust into blizzard of Lydian-flavored (in C: C D E F♯ G A B) scale passages, beginning at 1:38. Joe plays alternating bars of C and C5(♯11/9) chords, which contributes to the nebulous mood.

Joe returns to terra firma briefly at 2:38 for some blues-based eighth- and 16th-note figures. This is as close as we get to standard blues playing and accessible chords. During bars 5-13 of this section (2:35–3:02), Joe plays a passage that sounds like Larry Carlton doing a blues thing. At bar 14, though, it's all Joe, as he whips into a G Dorian flurry (G A B♭ C D E F) that signals we've gone aloft once more. Joe takes us out on the somnambulant melody line heard in the beginning of the tune.

FRIENDS

This is a country/major-flavored funker that immediately calls to mind Eric Johnson or Steve Morse. There's that epic, soaring quality to the lines, and the perfect mixture of linear fluidity and blues-based soul. At 0:28, the melody enters, based out of 14th-position D pentatonic major (D E F♯ A B). At 1:13, the first guitar break occurs, with Joe working in the stratosphere (1st string, 17th fret and upwards). At bar 5 (1:24), he begins a country-flavored passage, complete with a major-6th arpeggio lick (bar 6, beat 2). At 1:44, Joe plays eight bars of cadenza-like sequences, working his way up the neck with slurred 32nd notes until he breaks into the bent, held-note blues figure in the sixth bar, and then finally to the climax phrase at bar 7.

ICE 9

If Joe Satriani was ever tapped to donate a theme song for a secret-agent movie, he would do well to contribute "Ice 9." With its pulsing eighth-note groove, minor tonalities and sinister melodies, "Ice 9" creates a mood of musical menace. The opening melody consists of short, melodic bursts surrounded by rests. This lets the groove shine through and makes the notes in the melody linger with maximum resonance. This is in high contrast to the solo sections, which are virtuosic and non-melodic in character. Take, for example, Guitar solo I, which kicks off with six bars of unrelenting rhythmic torture before it lands on the long tones of bars 7 and 8, only to endure the further harassment from the whammy bar.

Guitar solo II is a nightmare of effects, from bar machinations to irregular tuplet groupings to harmonics. These techniques often stack up on each other, creating simultaneous effects. For the quintessential example in compound effects, look at the backwards-recorded guitar solo (Guitar solo III) beginning at 1:55: At bar 6, Joe performs his famous "lizard down the throat" sound, by depressing the bar while gradually sliding the left hand up the neck. The hard part is trying to maintain a stationary pitch, but that's when the technique is most effective: you hear no change in the note's pitch, but there is something definitely *weird* going on there.

THE MIGHTY TURTLE HEAD

Joe riffs out in heavy fashion here, creating a Hendrix-like sound with his low-note thrusts and high-note stabs. Visions of "All Along The Watchtower" are clearly in evidence, especially in the section where Joe plays the repeated-note figures (beginning at the first double bar, 1:01).

Joe continues the Hendrix tribute at the solo (2:21) by playing blues-based lines and wide bends. Check out the bend and timed release in bar 3 for a particularly Hendrix-like gesture.

THE MYSTICAL POTATO HEAD GROOVE THING

As the title somewhat suggests, this is indeed a groove-tune-meets-something-exotic. After laying down aggressive, sputtery 16th-note riffs, Joe enters with the lead guitar playing an E harmonic minor–based line (E F♯ G A B C D♯). A skittish melody appears that is neither blues nor major nor minor. It's, well, quirky.

Quirky gives way to positively loopy at 1:33, where Joe plays a rapid-fire series of left-hand taps, while crossing his right hand over the left hand to mute the strings. Work up to the record's tempo slowly, or you may pull a muscle.

At 2:30, Joe combines this wide-interval arpeggio with an eight-bar passage of steady 16th notes. The figure is a set pattern of six notes—G, A, G, E, E, E—that takes three beats to rotate so that the starting note begins on the downbeat. Therefore, using the lowest common denominator of three and four (the number of beats per measure), you'll see that this pattern gets back to starting position (with the first G on beat 1) 12 beats—or a full three bars—later. This fascinating aspect of three-against-four produces a syncopation of sorts—it shifts the pattern around to unexpected parts of the beat.

At Rhythm Figure 6 (2:59), Joe begins his most eclectic passage yet: a tapping passage and repeated note section, peppered with bluesy figures. At this blazing tempo (♩=176) Joe still manages a subtle trick when playing the 16th-note sextuplets: He taps and slides with his pick's edge at the beginning of each grouping. After this, the rest of the song—which still reads like a compendium of unorthodox guitar techniques—is a veritable cakewalk.

RUBINA

The opening harmonics in this gentle song have an almost massless, ether-like feel to them. Joe keeps this two-guitar texture going until the end, supported by drums and assorted hand percussion instruments. The melody, which enters at 0:48, is an easy, G major-based line that employs Latin-sounding syncopation. At bar 9 he plays a second theme, which he then harmonizes in 4ths and 3rds—again evoking a Latin mood. Note there is an absence of electric guitar techniques—no bends or bar work, only subtle vibrato.

At 2:02, Joe shifts gears, timbrally speaking, and brings in a distorted guitar. The techniques change, too, as Joe goes more "electric." Now there's harmonics, bar work, palm mutes, more pronounced vibrato, and bends. He goes all out at 2:51, unleashing a cascade of slurred notes in rapid, cadenza-like rhythms. Of the 39 notes picked in that first bar, only four are picked with the right hand. Joe's playing throughout this song represents—on one level—a progression of techniques. He begins with conventional guitar techniques, ones that could be played on an acoustic or classical. After the double bar, he moves to standard electric-guitar techniques—bends, bar work, palm mutes. Finally, at 2:51 he progresses to the modern electric-guitar techniques that include long slurred passages and irregular tuplet groupings.

SATCH BOOGIE

Joe first grinds out a low-note riff that serves as the bedrock for this up-tempo boogie. He then heaps a bunch of chordal and single-line work over this, which at various times recalls Billy Gibbons, Eddie Van Halen, Stevie Ray Vaughan, and Jeff Beck. Immediately after the initial statement of the low-note groove, Joe launches head-long into his first solo: a non-melodic, lick-laden frenzy. Check out Joe's take on the famous Jimmy Page lick at bars 13-14. The standard version features a bent 3rd string on the 7th fret, followed by successive 5th-fret notes on the 2nd and 1st strings. Joe's variation makes it a rhythmic rotation, where a three-note lick is placed in a meter divisible by two and four. This creates instant syncopation, thereby raising the funk factor. The rapid ascension in 25-26 recalls Steve Morse, except that Joe slurs many of these notes where Steve would pick them.

The infamous section in this piece begins at 1:50, and involves Joe's longest tapping passage on record. He performs without a net, too: Bass and drums drop out completely and the only help is some stripped-down drums keeping the time. The fluidity in which Joe executes this passage of extended taps and slurs is even more impressive when you consider it's all performed on the 5th string. Joe also employs his *pitch axis* approach as his harmonic scheme. Pitch axis is where one note is kept as the tonic, in this case A, and a number of different modes are generated from it. For example, beginning at bar 20 (2:12), Joe plays successive two-bar phrases of A minor (A B C D E F G), A harmonic minor (A B C D E F G#), A Mixolydian (A B C# D E F# G), and A Lydian (A B C# D# E F# G#). "Satch Boogie" is a great example of the freedom with which Joe enjoys in his lead playing, and the organization and order he applies when approaching the structure of his pieces.

SUMMER SONG

Joe's groove for this song is based on an A5-D/A progression. The D/A is sort of a notational compromise. Joe actually plays a chord with D F# A and G, and he envisions it more as a Gmaj9/A. The unchanging bass note, A, becomes a pedal tone. (A pedal tone is an unchanging note over which a series of harmonies is placed.) The first melodic figure is played entirely with natural harmonics, aided by a precisely timed echo, which repeats the notes exactly one bar later. Joe then plays the main theme (0:25) with a healthy dose of wah juice. It's entirely diatonic to A Mixolydian (A B C# D E F# G), even when the above-mentioned A5-to-D/A progression changes to one which includes B5 and G5 chords. At 0:48, Joe plays the basic melody again, this time an octave higher. Now he's getting bolder with the variations, introducing longer bends and prolonged departures from the actual melody. Perhaps the neatest trick in this section occurs at bar 8, where Joe seamlessly incorporates the harmonic figure heard in the intro.

At 1:12 Joe introduces a new section, and leaves the warm confines of A major. Now he plays bluesy, rock figures and draws exclusively from A pentatonic blues (A C D E G), and then later A minor (A B C D E F G).

The solo begins conventionally, with eighth notes and accessible bends, but soon Joe progresses to a passage of 16th-notes and wide-interval pull-offs, so any hope of tracing a melody is dashed. He caps off this section with a heart-stopping single-note riff (2:05), draws a breath (musically speaking) by employing some long rhythms, and then delivers another jaw-dropper, at 2:14, beginning on the 1st string, 17th fret (high A, bent to B). This is one of Joe's great talents: He can play melodically and lyrically, and then rip your head off with a dazzling display of virtuosity, and then jump right back in the groove like it never happened. And while he's grinning at you non-chalantly, you're trying to pick your jaw up from your shoes and stuff your heart back in your chest.

SURFING WITH THE ALIEN

Joe puts a new spin on the classic surf beat in this song from the album of the same title. The lead guitar's strange tone is derived in part from a wah wah pedal turned on but not manipulated during playing. It's used strictly as a tone filter. Listen especially to Joe's use of harmonics as a means of coloring sustained melody notes. Also note his trem bar manipulations, which are controlled and precise, with no spillover into subsequent phrases. You'll notice a preponderance of quarter-tone bends as well. This is an effective means of giving a note a little "squeeze"—not so much as to change the pitch as to infuse the note with a little tension, a sense of movement.

The first truly strange-sounding technique comes at the modulation to C# minor (1:09). Joe achieves the "electric mosquito" effect by tapping with his pick edge very high on the neck in a two-note, tap-pull combination that repeats for five bars. Harmonically, it's in C# Phrygian-Dominant (Joe's name for the 5th mode of F# harmonic minor: F# G# A B C# D E#). Because of the various tuplet rhythmic groupings, it really amounts to a trill. He breaks out of it at bar 5 with a long, fast passage in F# minor (F# G# A B C# D E). After a slower, eight-bar interlude in D# minor (six sharps, whew!), Joe plays a fast but stationary passage in F minor, before launching into some soaring and scary-sounding bends.

Then it seems to "open up" into a country-sounding G major passage (though the key signature tells us we're in G minor). There's a brief re-cap of the original melody but with a twist: After the four-bar jet-plane sample, another extended break of pulls and trem-bar-manipulated notes surfaces. This is followed by double stops in jerky, dotted rhythms, a tapping section, and more fun with the bar wreaking havoc over melody notes. At the fade Joe repeats the original melodic idea harmonized in thirds.

This piece is a compendium of modern rock techniques, and what's nice is that because of the insistent groove, you get to see how Joe employs these tricks in a rhythmic context. It's easy to use the bar in an arhythmic situation or to let feedback do its thing by letting it ring for days, but Joe's gift is his ability to bring all these techniques to bear inside a groove taken at a fierce clip. That's why Joe hangs ten with the supernatural.

TABLATURE: A six-line staff that graphically represents the guitar fingerboard. By placing a number on the appropriate line, the string and the fret of any note can be indicated. For example:

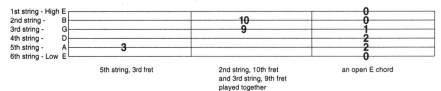

| 1st string - High E |
| 2nd string - B |
| 3rd string - G |
| 4th string - D |
| 5th string - A |
| 6th string - Low E |

5th string, 3rd fret

2nd string, 10th fret
and 3rd string, 9th fret
played together

an open E chord

Definitions for Special Guitar Notations

BEND: Strike the note and bend up ½ step (one fret).

BEND: Strike the note and bend up a whole step (two frets).

BEND AND RELEASE: Strike the note and bend up ½ (or whole) step, then release the bend back to the original note. All three notes are tied; only the first note is struck.

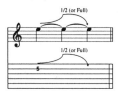

PRE-BEND: Bend the note up ½ (or whole) step, then strike it.

PRE-BEND AND RELEASE: Bend the note up ½ (or whole) step, strike it and release the bend back to the original note.

UNISON BEND: Strike the two notes simultaneously and bend the lower note to the pitch of the higher.

VIBRATO: Vibrate the note by rapidly bending and releasing the string with a left-hand finger.

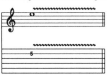

WIDE OR EXAGGERATED VIBRATO: Vibrate the pitch to a greater degree with a left-hand finger or the tremolo bar.

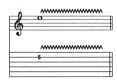

SLIDE: Strike the first note and then with the same left-hand finger move up the string to the second note. The second note is not struck.

SLIDE: Same as above, except the second note is struck.

SLIDE: Slide up to the note indicated from a few frets below.

HAMMER-ON: Strike the first (lower) note, then sound the higher note with another finger by fretting it without picking.

PULL-OFF: Place both fingers on the notes to be sounded. Strike the first (higher) note, then sound the lower note by pulling the finger off the higher note while keeping the lower note fretted.

TRILL: Very rapidly alternate between the note indicated and the small note shown in parentheses by hammering on and pulling off.

TAPPING: Hammer ("tap") the fret indicated with the right-hand index or middle finger and pull off to the note fretted by the left hand.

NATURAL HARMONIC: With a left-hand finger, lightly touch the string over the fret indicated, then strike it. A chime-like sound is produced.

ARTIFICIAL HARMONIC: Fret the note normally and sound the harmonic by adding the right-hand thumb edge or index finger tip to the normal pick attack.

TREMOLO BAR: Drop the note by the number of steps indicated, then return to original pitch.

PALM MUTE: With the right hand, partially mute the note by lightly touching the string just before the bridge.

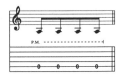

MUFFLED STRINGS: Lay the left hand across the strings without depressing them to the fret-board; strike the strings with the right hand, producing a percussive sound.

PICK SLIDE: Rub the pick edge down the length of the string to produce a scratchy sound.

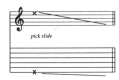

TREMOLO PICKING: Pick the note as rapidly and continuously as possible.

RHYTHM SLASHES: Strum chords in rhythm indicated. Use chord voicings found in the fingering diagrams at the top of the first page of the transcription.

SINGLE-NOTE RHYTHM SLASHES: The circled number above the note name indicates which string to play. When successive notes are played on the same string, only the fret numbers are given.

Always With Me, Always With You

Music by Joe Satriani

*Gtr. III tuned to "Nashville tuning;" ⑥ - ③ stgs. are tuned one octave higher than normal.

*Two guitars. Upstemmed part is played on "Nashville" tuned
electric; fingerings shown here are for guitar in standard tuning.
See Riff A for fingerings and positions used in "Nashville" tuning.

Big Bad Moon

Words and Music by
Joe Satriani

† Attack stgs w/edge of pick, starting above bridge
pickup and moving down towards the nut.
Pitches shown are arbitrary.

When the night falls,__ the big moon's gon - na rise.

__ (w/echo repeats)   You can look right up,   see it   in __ the sky.__

Makes me feel_ like I'm gon-na blow_ a fuse. _____ (w/echo repeats)

I start to shiv - er and shake with a strange kind_ of blues_ (w/echo repeats)

(Half time feel)
Chorus

(Spoken) But I like it. __

Gtr.
I

pick slides - - - -
(w/Wah wah)

Gtr.
II

trem. bar
pick slides - - - - - - - - - - -

(Double-time feel)
Guitar solo I
w/Rhy. Fig. 1 (8 times)

8va- loco

semi-
harm.

reverse rake - -

2nd Verse
w/Rhy. Fig. 3 (8 times) & Fill 1

see it now,— the moon is high— a - bove.— *(w/echo repeats)* It's got a

hold on me,— but I just can't get— e - nough.— *(w/echo repeats)*

Big, round, black and— white,— I feel the pull,— I see— the light.—

w/ad lib vocal

Big bad moon's look - ing down on me— to - night.— *(w/echo repeats)*

(Half time feel)
Chorus

(Spoken) But I like it.

Rhy. Fig. 3

Fill 1

Fill 2
(Gtr. IV)

*Lightly touch stg. at 21 fr. while holding A (③ 14 fr.).

When the moon comes,__ got no - where_ to hide. *(w/echo repeats)*

It can turn your head a - round_____ like it turns_ the tide._ *(w/echo repeats)*

Man, wom - an, boy,_ child._ Make you feel_ like_ you were

born__ wild._ Big bad moon's look - ing down on me_ to - night._

(Spoken) But I like it._

Circles

Music by Joe Satriani

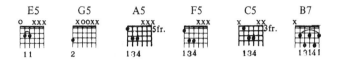

The Crush Of Love

Music by Joe Satriani

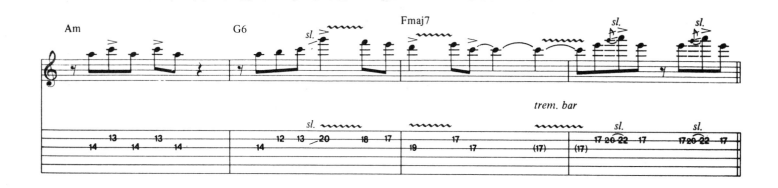

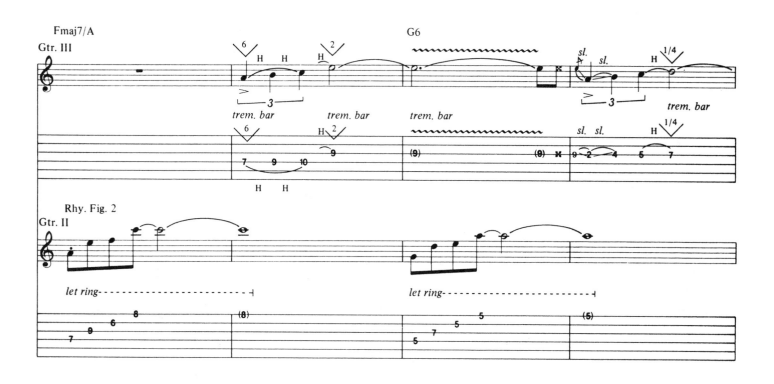

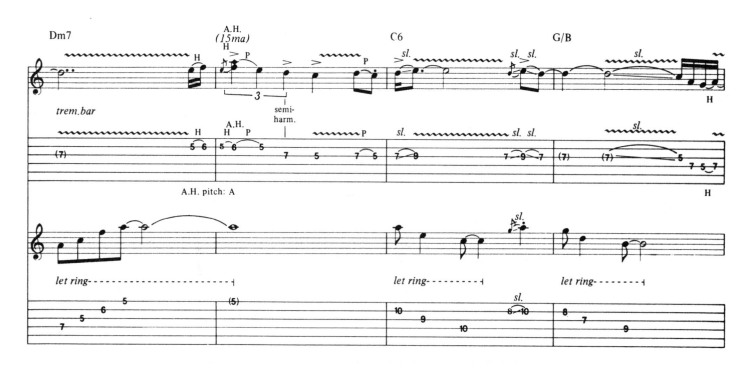

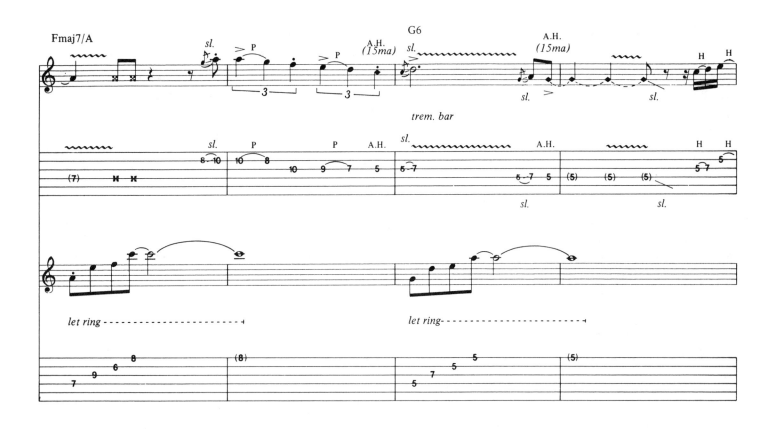

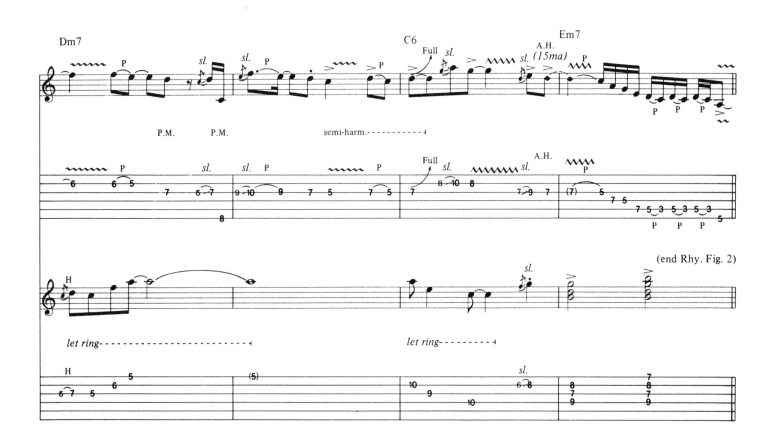

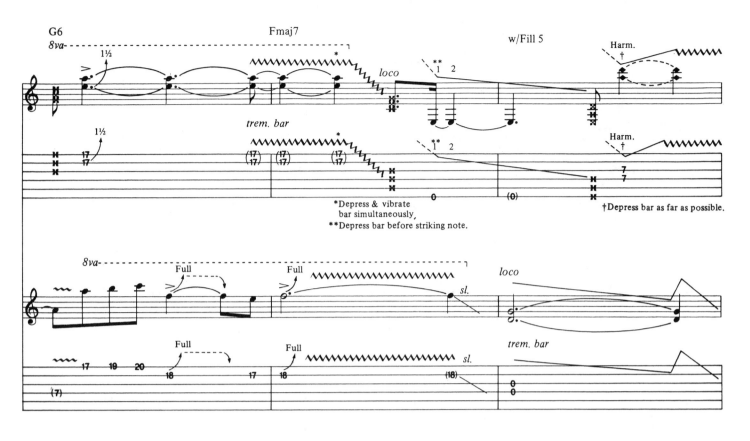

*Depress & vibrate
bar simultaneously.
**Depress bar before striking note.

†Depress bar as far as possible.

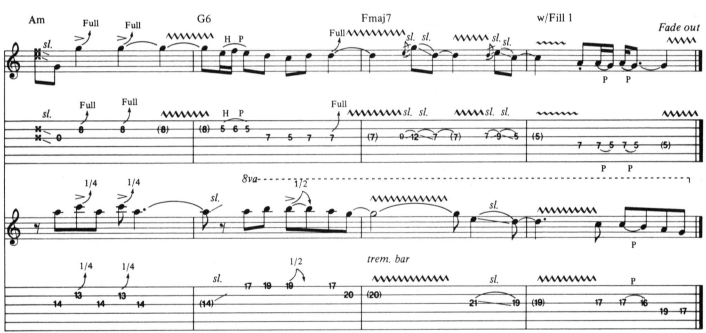

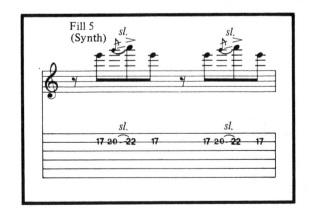

Cryin'

Music by Joe Satriani

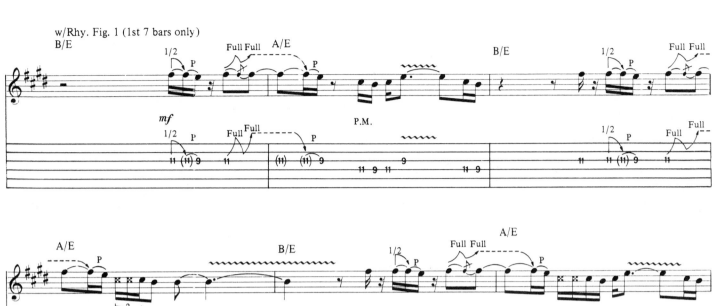

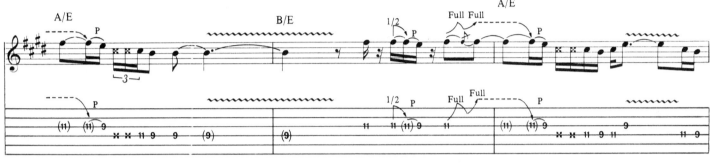

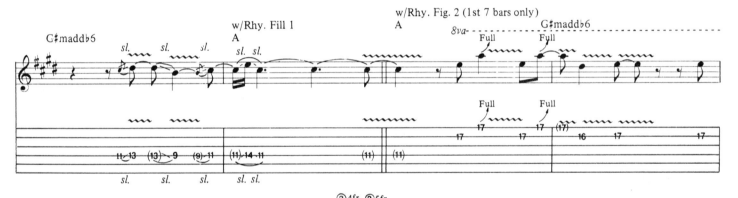

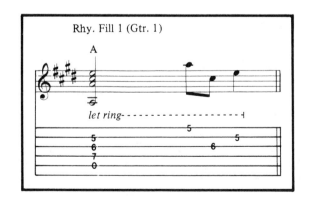

Flying In A Blue Dream

Music by Joe Satriani

48

*Tap and slide with edge of pick throughout this measure.

w/Rhy. Fig. 2 (2 times)

*Pull up on bar.

w/Rhy. Fig. 1 (6 times)

*Pull up on bar.

*Pull up on bar.

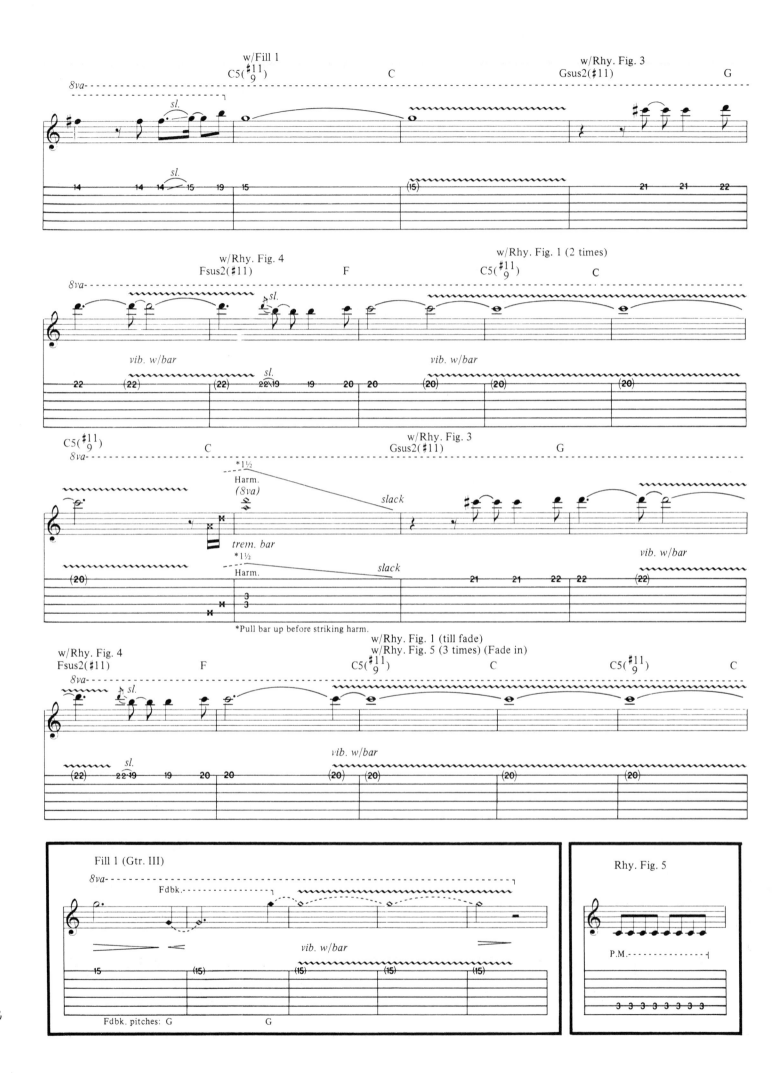

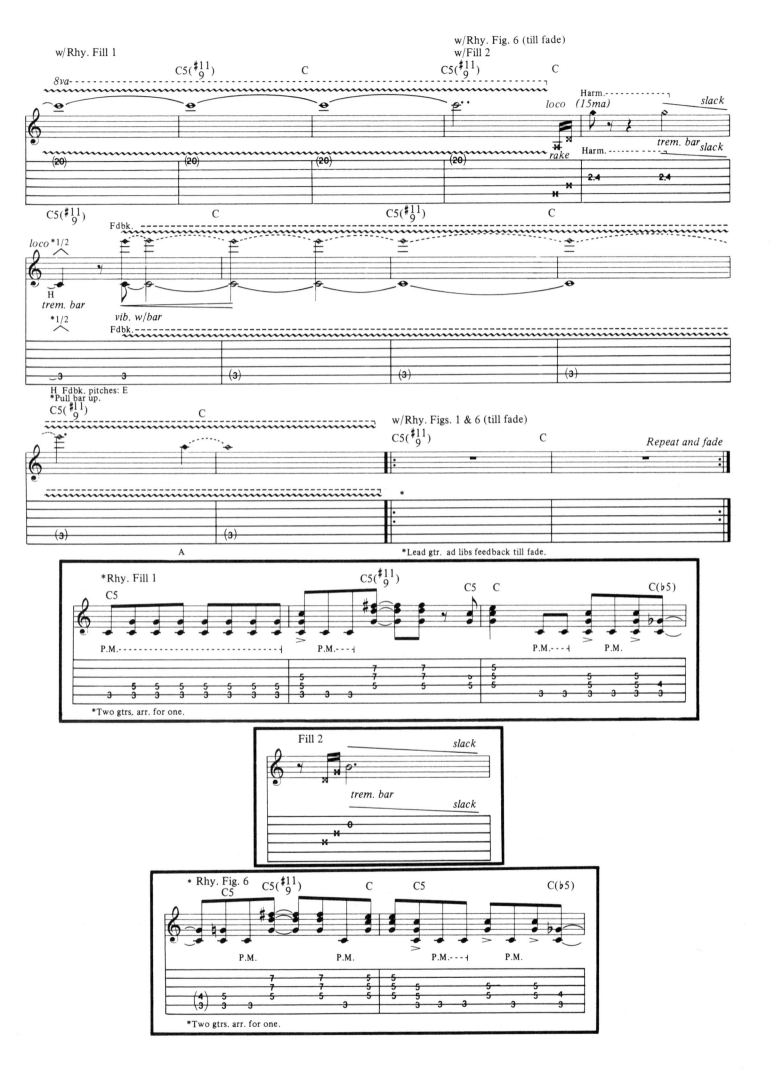

Friends

Music by Joe Satriani
and Andy Johns

56

58

Ice 9

Music by Joe Satriani

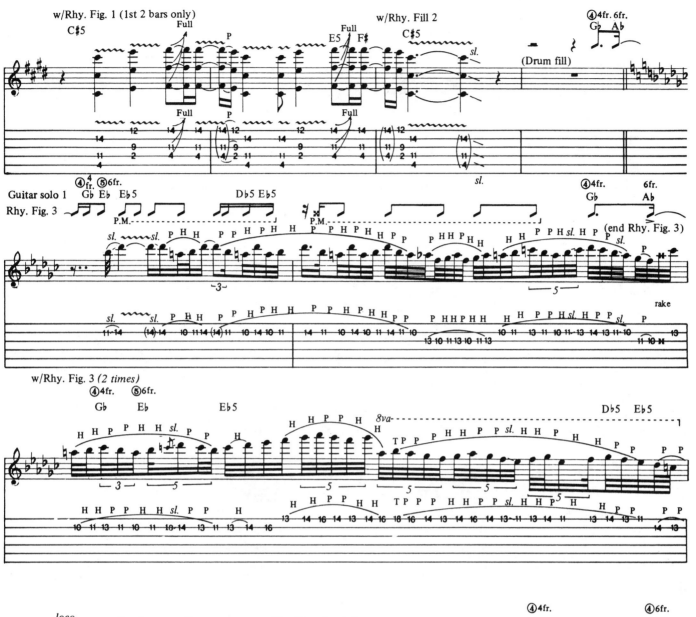

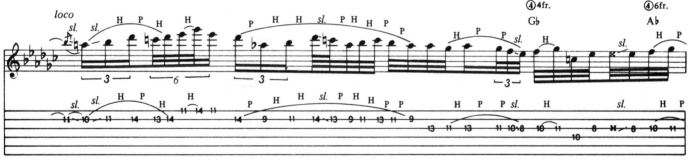

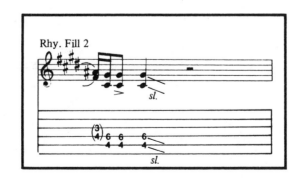

**Slide pick down stg. over bridge pickup. †Depress bar while gradually sliding up (or release while sliding down), approximately maintaining solitary pitch; press hard while sliding to make fret sound as loud as possible. (Joe calls this the "lizard down the throat" sound).

††Rhy. Fill 3 replaces last bar of Rhy. Fig. 2 from this point till fade.

***Bend both notes w/3rd finger.

The Mighty Turtle Head

Music by Joe Satriani

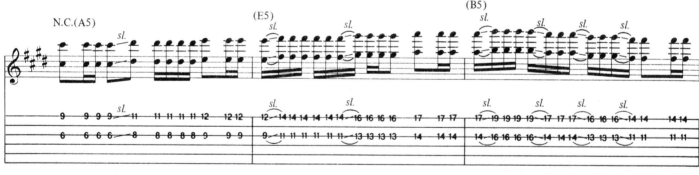

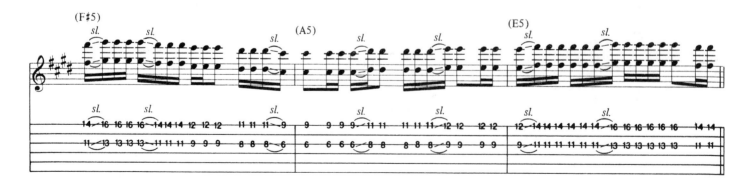

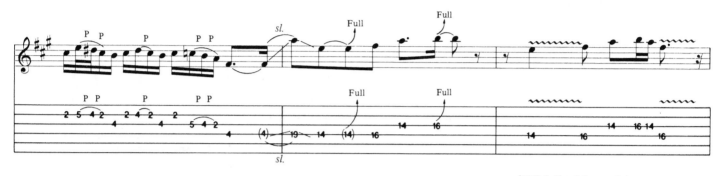

w/Riff A (1st 3 bars only)

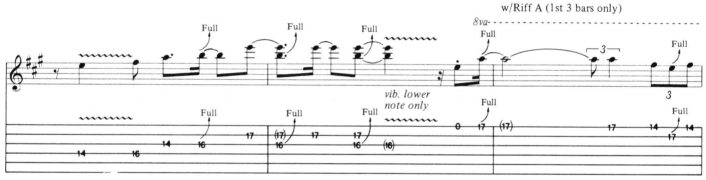

w/Rhy. Fill 1 (Gtr. I)

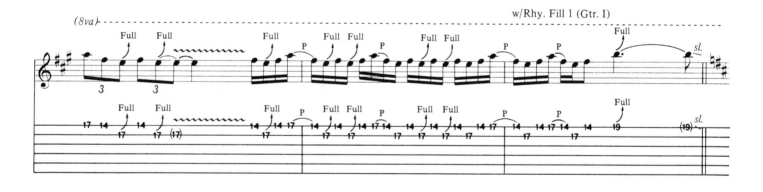

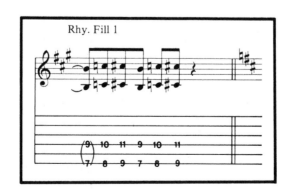

Rhy. Fill 1

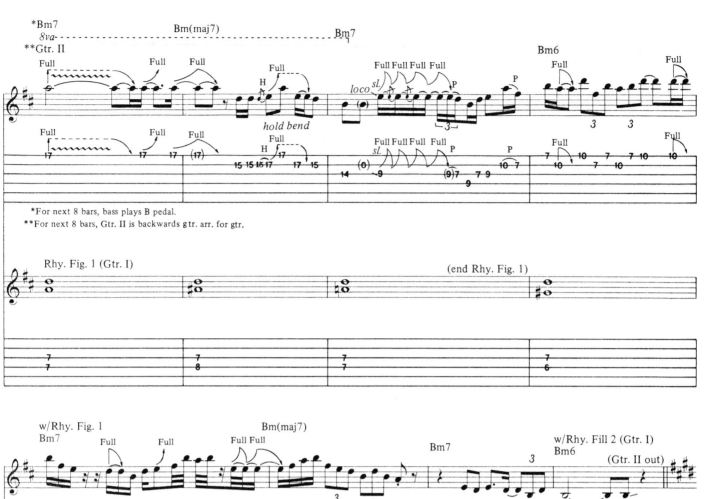

*For next 8 bars, bass plays B pedal.
**For next 8 bars, Gtr. II is backwards gtr. arr. for gtr.

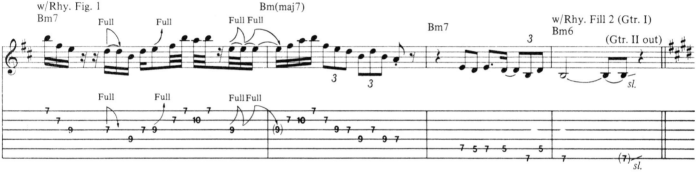

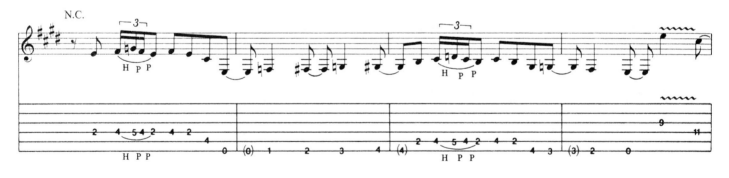

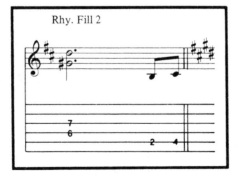

Rhy. Fill 2

*Chord played by synth (w/Mellotron effect) over next 10 bars as follows:
bars 1-2, root only; bars 3-4, add ♯4; bars 5-6, add 5th and 7th;
bars 7-10, add octave.

*Synth bent w/wheel up to C,
then down to A, then back up to B.

The Mystical Potato Head Groove Thing

Music by Joe Satriani

*Tap & slide w/edge of pick throughout next
4½ bars except where noted.

w/Rhy. Fig. 7 (3½ times)

*L.H. slide

Rhy. Fig. 7

*Tap w/edge of pick.

*Point bar backwards and bounce hand to produce each note.

Rubina

Music by Joe Satriani

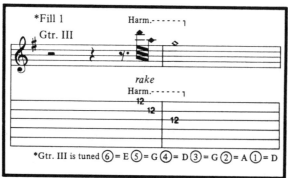

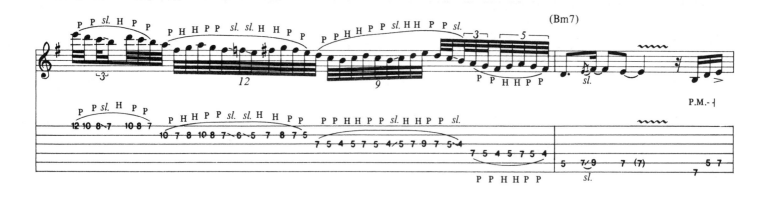

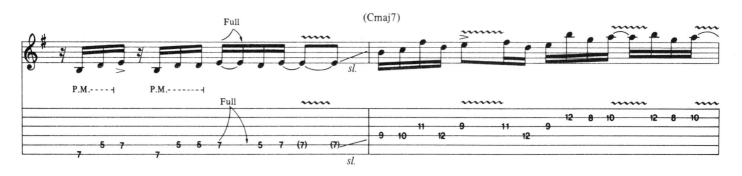

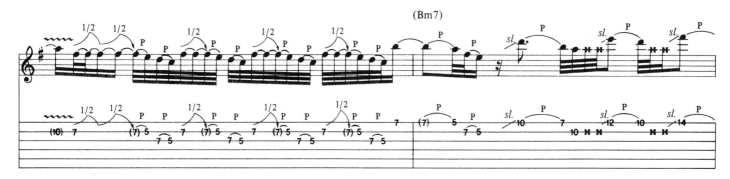

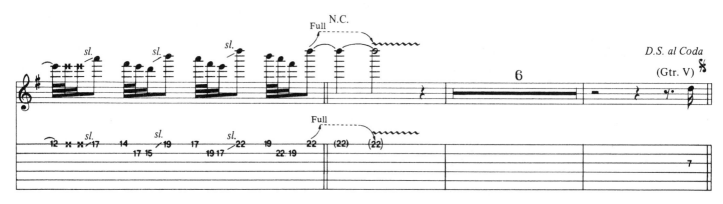

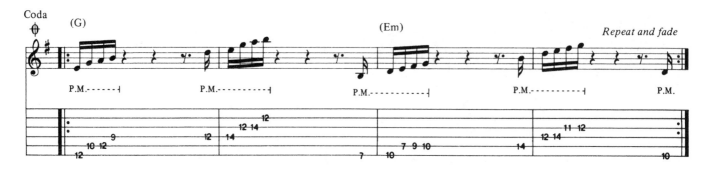

Satch Boogie

Music by Joe Satriani

Summer Song

Music by Joe Satriani

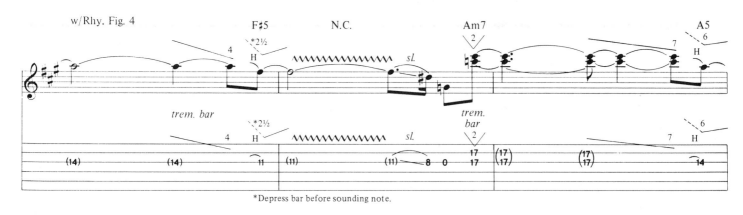

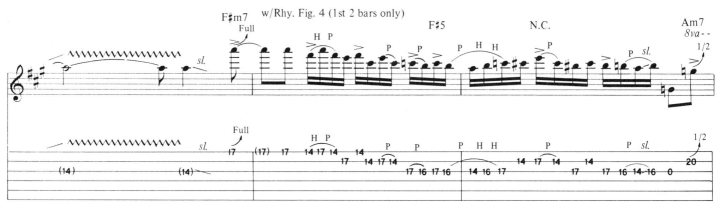

*Depress bar before sounding note.

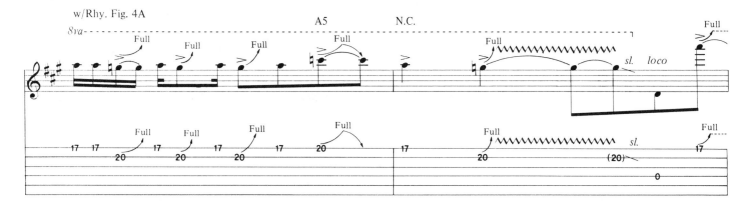

114

116

Surfing With The Alien

Music by Joe Satriani

CHERRY LANE

Presents

the Music of
JOE SATRIANI

Dreaming #11	**Time Machine: Book 2**
02506974	*02501227*
The Extremist	**5 Of The Best/**
02501205	*Volume 1*
	02506219
Flying In A Blue Dream	
02507029	**5 Of The Best/**
	Volume 2
Not Of This Earth	*02506236*
02507074	
	Riff By Riff
Surfing With The Alien	*02506314*
02506959	
	Guitar Secrets
Time Machine: Book 1	*02506305*
02501226	

Available from your local music dealer _____

EXCLUSIVELY DISTRIBUTED BY
HAL•LEONARD™ CORPORATION
7777 W. BLUEMOUND RD. P.O. BOX 13819 MILWAUKEE, WI 53213